Going from Zero to 778 Credit Score in 15 Months

Your 9 Step Guide to Saving Thousands When You Finance Your Next Home or Car

A Getting Started Guide for Those with Nothing on a Credit Report

LORETTA CROSBY

GOING FROM ZERO TO 778 CREDIT SCORE IN 15 MONTHS

Copyright © 2017 Loretta Crosby

All rights reserved.

The information in this document is protected by copyright. No part of this publication may be reprinted, copied, redistributed, retransmitted, hosted, displayed or stored electronically in whole or in part without the express written permission of the author.

The writer has no affiliation with any credit bureau or any of their contractual agencies. Information contained herein is not intended to provide exact or precise advice, and should not be construed as constituting legal advice.

The entire contents are opinions expressed by the author solely from personal experience. The author and publisher are not responsible for any errors or omissions and disclaim any liability whatsoever for personal loss caused by the use or misuse of or inability to use any or all of the information contained within this publication. Use this information at your own discretion and risk.

All company names and brand names are the property of their respective owners and are used in editorial commentary as permitted by law.

ISBN-13:978-1975850241
ISBN-10:1975850246

One Pupil Publications
PO BOX 573
GASTONIA NC 28053

Visit us online at
www.OnePupilPublications.com/books/

Dedicated to the Source of all my inspiration and desire to give and be of service to others.
YOU ROCK!

ZERO TO 778

CONTENTS

	Acknowledgments	i
1	Find and Join a Credit Union	1
2	Secure A Small Personal Loan	4
3	Apply for a Credit Card	7
4	Keep Tabs on Your Credit Score	11
5	Strike When the Iron is Hot	14
6	Do Not Overspend	20
7	Tithe to Something	23
8	Tithe to Yourself	26
9	Create Some Residual Income	30
10	Author's Story	35

ACKNOWLEDGMENTS

This little book that can change your financial future would not have been possible or conceived had I not gotten so many rejections in applying to buy a badly needed car with absolutely "no credit" or zero items on my credit report. I had been living in a "cash" economy ever since my first money meltdown that left messy stains on my report that had to come off in seven years. Thanks to the Nissan salesman who advised I join a credit union, and to the CreditKarma.com website that gave recommendations on how to proceed once my credit score started to rise.

STEP 1
FIND AND JOIN A CREDIT UNION

So there I was in April 2016 trying to get my 19-year-old 1997 Toyota Camry to pass its yearly inspection. The car had served me well since it was given to me in 2008, but it was steadily approaching the 300,000-mile odometer reading, and I suspected its days were numbered.

However, that is not something you say aloud and especially not while you are driving down the highway while inside the vehicle. The car has feelings, you know, and maybe even ears, so I kept those little observations very closely guarded and to myself.

That month, I visited a local Nissan dealership to test the waters, fully expecting to be turned down for a car loan.

The car salesperson was gentle, but frank with me as he broke the news to me. He told me my credit score was non-existent. I responded by telling him that I had lived in a "cash only" economy for many years now, but that my car was not going to last forever. Then I asked for his advice.

"What should I do?" I asked.

Though he was much younger than I was, he spoke to me as one would a younger sister. He told me that what I needed to do was to find a credit union to join and then try to get a secured credit card and maybe even open an account at a local department store. All this so that I could re-establish and rebuild my credit.

I had previously been a member of a credit union many years ago when I worked in state government, but I no longer had such affiliation. Still, I had recently seen a commercial advertising the Charlotte Metro Credit Union as a community credit union without the usual prerequisites.

So I made a Google search, signed up online, made a $300 opening deposit, and became a member by opening a checking account. Shortly thereafter, I inquired about getting a loan, one that I would secure by making a deposit to my savings account.

I talked to my personal credit union representative and told her my goal was to re-establish my credit.

How much should I deposit, and how long should the loan term be were questions I wanted answers to as I began my journey of climbing the credit-rebuilding mountain.

Step 1 -- Summary / To Do

Join a Near-By Credit Union

If you cannot meet the "affiliation" requirements to join a local credit union, consider using the internet to find a credit union that accepts members who might not otherwise qualify for membership. Apply for membership and join. Many credit unions require you to open a savings account and maintain a small balance to remain an active member. But you can handle it. Remember, this is your first step on a journey that can save you thousands of dollars on your next big purchase, so jump in and get started as soon as possible.

> "As for the Future, your task is not to foresee but to enable it."
>
> Antoine De Saint-Exupery

STEP 2
FIND THE MONEY TO
SECURE A SMALL PERSONAL LOAN

As someone who had no savings--at the time--I had to think about where the money would come from to secure the personal loan that I concluded needed to be an amount somewhere between $300 to $500.

As fate would have it, I had gotten a small income tax refund -- thanks to Obama Care -- as a tax credit for entrepreneurs.

But, even if that money had not been available, I would have asked a relative or a friend to loan me the money because my determination to secure the loan was strong. I knew my car was on its last leg and would have to be replaced in the not so distant future.

You may already have the money tucked away under your mattress or in a savings or checking account somewhere. It is important in this step to entrust the funds to your credit union for safekeeping.

Once I gave the Credit Union the money to secure the loan, the representative told me that I could pay the $500 back by simply deducting the money each month from the savings account they had created for me to place the funds. That way, she said, I would not have to worry about coming up with the six monthly payments, but instead could focus on other things as the money was paid back automatically.

Somehow, it seemed silly to have secured a $500 loan and not be able to "spend" or use the money on something or anything I chose.

The representative then told me that the other option was for her to give me the funds or transfer them to my checking account so that they were immediately available to me to use.

I choose the second option. In retrospect, I do not recall what I wanted the funds for, but seems like if you loan me money, I should have access to the capital. "Not a problem," she said.

So now, I had done at least two things that the car salesperson had suggested I do. The Credit Union, of course, would be reporting the new loan to the three major credit bureaus as well as reporting my repayment history.

I made sure I repaid the loan as agreed upon with no late payments -- no matter what.

In six months, I had repaid the loan and I could see that I now had a credit score.

In the meantime, I had also set up a free account at a website called CreditKarma.com so that I could keep up with my credit score for free.

Step 2 -- Summary / To Do

Apply for a Secured Personal Loan

Whether you use your tax refund, personal savings or borrow the funds from a friend or relative, applying for a personal loan through your credit union or other financial institution can put a line of credit on your credit score sheet. Generally, if you offer to secure the loan by leaving the monetary amount of the loan in the credit union or bank, you should have no problem with the organization granting you the personal secured loan. Your goal is to get the loan from an institution that will report your payments to the three major credit bureaus. The sooner the account is opened, the sooner the reporting can start.

> *"I have bad reflexes. I was once run over by a car being pushed by two guys."*
>
> Woody Allen

STEP 3
APPLY FOR A CREDIT CARD
(SECURED OR UNSECURED)

Everyone is aware or should be aware that when you are rebuilding credit, it is helpful to have various lines of credit on your credit report.

That might include having a personal loan, a credit card or two, maybe an automobile loan or a mortgage or department store credit account.

At six months after reentering the credit game and essentially exiting the "cash only" economy and mentality, I now had one account on my record. That personal loan was in good standing and now paid off. Wow. That was easy.

Credit Karma advised that there were certain credit card companies that I would have a good or fair chance at being approved for a secured credit card if I applied.

It was now November and approaching the

Christmas season, so once again I called my credit union representative. She said I would need proof of income, etcetera, when I made my application for the credit card.

Since I had no income outside of my monthly book royalties, I decided not to go that route because of all the hassle to document all the sources from which my income was derived. So instead, I applied for a credit card online through Capital One.

I chose Capital One because the company had acquired Ing Direct a few years back, and I had a checking account with the previous online banker for many years. I chose them also because their sales literature said they would start you off with a small line of credit and then up the amount in six months if you made your payments on time and kept your account in good standing.

So, I applied and received an unsecured line of credit for $300 big ones. Whew. Now I had Capital One reporting my timely payments to the three credit bureaus, and two accounts in total on my credit file. My credit score kept rising. It was now in the high 500s. Amazing.

Then a friend told me about something called Care Credit, a company that gives you credit to pay for certain medical expenses. I needed glasses, and I needed some dental work, so late one night while surfing the net, I applied for a credit card from them.

The application asked how much I needed and I

entered in $3,000. I was instantly approved. No income verification requested or required. Okay, now we are "cooking with oil," as we say in the Carolinas.

Then, when they sent me my card, I saw the 26.99 % yearly interest rate and decided that I could not in good conscious use the card unless and until I could afford to pay off any subsequent bill.

The new teeth on both sides of my mouth would have to wait. The eyeglasses would have to wait. How long? I did not know.

So now, I had three lines of credit reported on my credit file, and not using the $3000 from the Care Credit card was helping to keep my percentage of credit usage down, which was a factor that also helped to increase my overall credit score.

Now my score had climbed to over 650 and I was ecstatic. What could be better? I could buy Christmas gifts and use the new card from Capital to pay utility bills and keep my payments current.

I was starting to enjoy this new "building credit score" game.

Step 3 -- Summary / To Do

Apply for a Credit Card

If you already have a bank account at an institution that offers secured or unsecured credit cards, applying for a credit card through that bank might prove advantageous. They may offer you an unsecured card based on your past history as a customer with them. If, however, that is not an option, you can always Google to find an organization that does offer a secured card.

In the alternative, you can use the information provided in the next step to find a credit card company that you would have favorable odds of having your application approved based on the credit score you now have. Do this after your secured personal loan has been paid off.

> " *Consider that people are like tea bags. They don't know their own strength until they get into hot water.*"
>
> **Dan McKinnon**

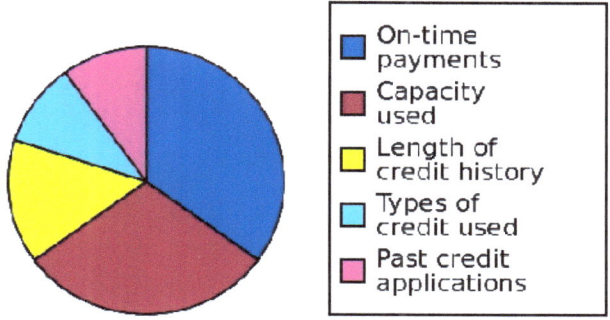

STEP 4
KEEP TABS ON YOUR CREDIT SCORE

Online websites like CreditKarma.com make it easy to keep up with your credit score, and all at no out of pocket cost to you.

All you do is signup, login and look. They even send you email notices when your score changes for any reason

Of course, there is no such thing as a free lunch, and I suspect that the way they make their money off registrants is by promoting different offers to help you rebuild your credit or by promoting other offers from loan companies that provide services you might be in the market for.

Let's face it. You do not need credit if you are not looking to finance something. So yes, they have car loans and mortgage links to use when you are ready for such services. Still, I found them to be unintrusive and unpushy whenever I log in to check my scores monthly.

What I really like about the free service is their "credit simulator" function, which allows you to see the potential impact that certain actions would have on your credit if they existed. For instance, would your credit score go up or down if you took out a new loan, opened a new line of credit, or were hit with a new collection on your report?

Monitoring your credit score helps you know when you have reached another milestone in your credit worthiness (as measured by the data collectors).

This allows you to Google a particular score to find out what favorable interest rates you might qualify for when you are in the market for big-ticket items such as cars and mortgages.

In essence, it allows you to time your purchases so that the most favorable interest rates are available to you.

And that is the reason you need to monitor your score. Plus, when you watch your score steadily rise, it gives you incentive to keep up the good work, to keep paying your bills on time, and to try not to use all the credit you have so your percentage of usage is low as you continue to build the numbers.

Step 4 -- Summary / To Do

Find a website that allows you monthly access to your credit report, preferably a free service.

Use the reminders you get from your credit score website to periodically check your credit score at least once a month. Play around with the credit score stimulator -- if you have access to one -- to determine if one or more small actions recommended might positively affect your score. Try to space out your little actions. Remember there is no rush to climb this little credit score mountain, so remain calm and keep rowing the boat.

STEP 5
STRIKE WHEN THE IRON IS HOT:
BUY SOMETHING WHEN YOUR SCORE
GOES ABOVE 700

Now it's June 2017. And I have been playing the "build your credit score" game for a little over a year.

Credit Karma is showing me a score of 677 and I'm feeling frisky. I am also feeling very warm without air conditioning in my 1997 Toyota. A couple of summers without air conditioning, a couple of winters without heat inside the vehicle and I'm feeling that waiting another summer to try and finance a car would be a bit much.

Intuitively I start to feel the nudge to start shopping for a car. Never mind I was only working 12-14 hours a week making "small small" money as they would say in Ghana. I wanted to have a new ride before my 60th so that would give me three months to shop around and find a deal.

What I did not anticipate was that car salespersons do not want you waiting three months; they want to sell you now.

After visiting only two big dealerships and a few small ones, I had already fallen in love with the 2012 Nissan Murano. Luckily for me, it was more than what my budget allowed.

I use the word "budget" loosely because as a student of the law of attraction, if the truth be told, I really did not have a budget for a new or used car at any price.

But I wanted that Murano.

So I decided on a budget based on a new business idea that I was working on. And not knowing how much higher my credit score would go, I decided the 677 would be enough to get me a decent interest rate on a used car.

Once again, I went online and applied for an auto loan through my new partner in finance -- the Charlotte Metro Credit Union.

When they finally contacted me about three weeks later, I was not expecting "favor".

After all, it had taken them three weeks to respond which was not their customary customer service. By this time, I was almost expecting a letter of denial to come in the mail.

When I did get the call, as it turned out, they said they had been working on trying to extend the term of the loan so that my requested payment terms could be met.

But because three weeks had already passed, I only had seven days to find a car based on the credit score they had approved me on. I later learned that score was 703.

My gut told me I should try my best to find a car within that time limit, and so I began my search.

Unlike traditional car hunters, I decided to chuck going from car dealership to car dealership and test driving their inventory.

Instead, I decided to let the car come to me. I spoke to the universe and decided to put the word out that I was seeking a dependable, reliable used car and that someone I knew who knew someone could and would fulfill my need in the easiest way.

One night as I was closing the shop at my "day job", there was a young man who I told that I was in the market for a new used car, to which he replied: "My brother is the sales manager at (XYZ) dealership." Bingo. Let the games begin!

The next day, I went to the dealership, asked to speak to the sales manager by name, told him the type of vehicle I desired, how much I wanted to pay for it, and that I had my financing secured, and asked him if he could meet that need.

I have to admit I had a certain level of trust going in because I worked with his younger brother.

After a brief discussion, with him trying to convince me to finance through the dealership resources, he said, "I have just the car in mind for you."

And it was just the car for me. A little bigger SUV than I wanted to drive, not a Murano, but it was a clean, very clean one local owner vehicle, 10 years old, 91,000 miles and most importantly, it had air-conditioning!

I test drove that car, and the next day I took it to my mechanic so he could eyeball it, made the purchase, then drove my new used car out of town and enjoyed every minute of the ride to a function in another state that same day.

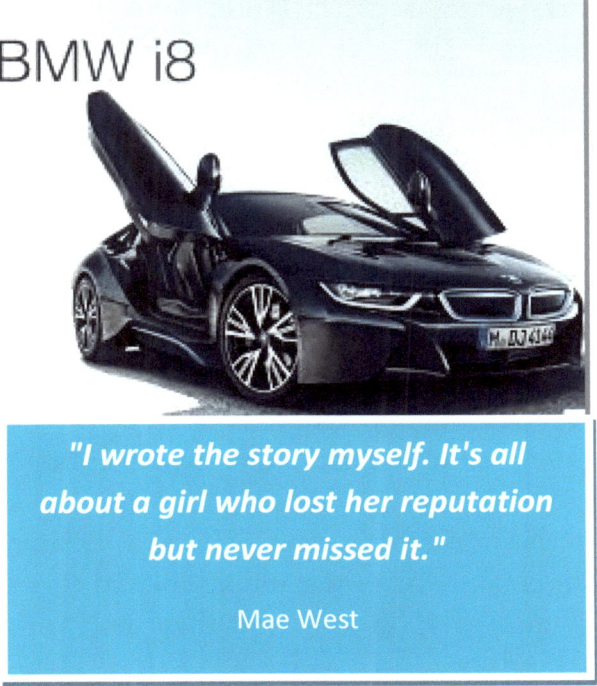

Step 5 -- Summary / To Do

Buy Something When Your Credit Score Gets to the 700 Milestone

What I learned from the salesperson at the dealership was that those online credit scores you get can be 50 to 60 points below what your actual score shows. The other thing I learned from the transaction was never switch sides when you already have your financing in place. By being talked into financing through the dealership, they send your information to six to eight different lenders, and those hard inquiries can have a negative impact on your credit score.

Without going into a lot of detail, switching lenders in the middle of the game turned out to be disastrous for me, with me receiving a phone call five days after the sale, and the finance manager at the car dealership telling me the lender was not willing to finance the transaction because my income was not sufficient to support the purchase, plus he said they were treating me like I was new to the credit scene and really had not established enough credit history. That's why it is important to develop a relationship with your credit union. They are known for being more lenient with their members and more willing to take a chance on you, and they will work with you to get it done.

But long story short, I ended up going to my credit union to pick up the check to pay for my five-day-old purchase, getting some extra perks while at the credit union, like a four year extended power train type warranty on the 10-year-old car, and a new credit card as part of the deal. You can read more details in the next chapter.

But with that story aside, the thing you have to do is go out and buy something with your new, over 700 credit score. After all, you are not just building your score for the fun of it. You are building it to get lower interest rates on your big-ticket purchases.

While buying a car was my test purchase, and I felt the time was right to do so, you may want to wait until your score grows even larger before attempting your first major purchase. That will be up to you and your wallet.

.

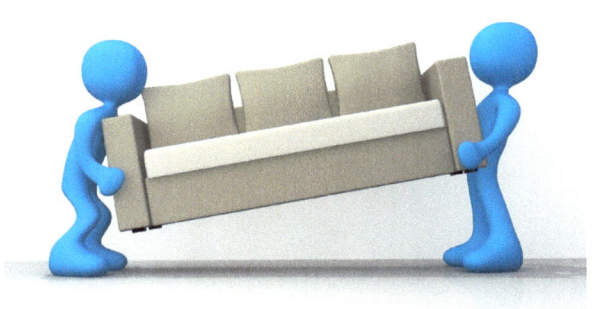

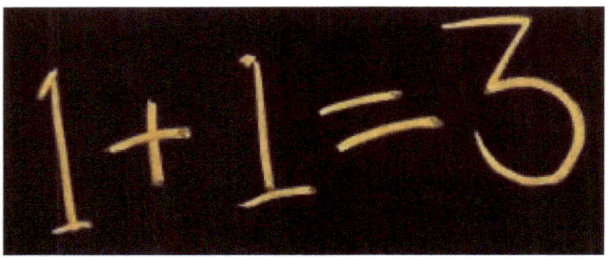

STEP 6
DO NOT OVERSPEND
BUDGETING IS KEY

You read the last chapter, and I hope you noticed that I talked about making a budget for the new expense. It's important that you know how much you can afford to put out monthly on a new bill or purchase before you go out and create the new bill. If you do not do this, there is the high possibility that you will over extend yourself and end up in the same credit score hole that you just spent a year trying to correct.

There are some agencies that can help you learn to budget when you get in over your head, but the best preventive measure is to know your limitations before you start hunting for the new house or the new car.

Budgeting has always come easy for me and has never been a problem for me. My problem has always been not earning or having enough money to afford the things I desire. For me, it's the price of living a simple life on my own terms.

Many years back when I was having financial problems -- I was facing foreclosure on my condominium -- I remember talking to a credit counselor and giving her my budget. After reviewing it, she told me that they could not help me do a better job with the money I had to work with then I was already doing myself.

So if you need help in budgeting and not overspending on your next big ticket item purchase, go out and find it before you make the purchase. It could save you untold and unnecessary headaches in the long run.

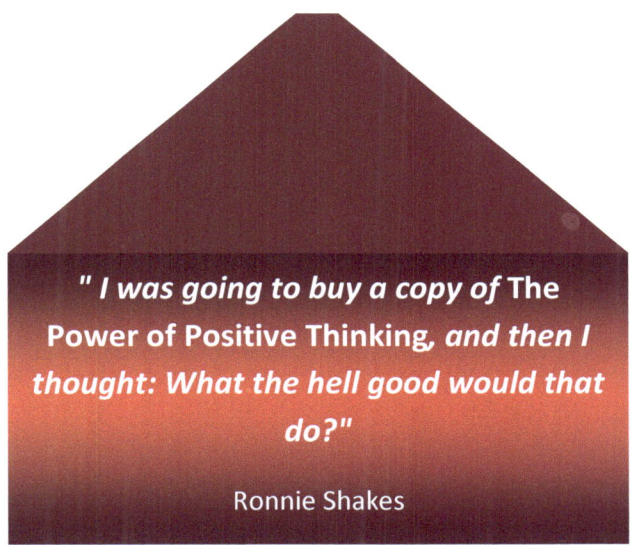

" *I was going to buy a copy of* The Power of Positive Thinking, *and then I thought: What the hell good would that do?*"

Ronnie Shakes

Step 6 -- Summary / To Do

Make a Budget for Your Purchases Before You Buy

If budgeting is not one of your strong points, there are many non-profit credit-counseling agencies that are willing to help you create and manage a budget that you would be able to live with. Seek one out if you are at all hesitant about your ability to repay a loan. Ideally, you would seek out help before the purchase is made or postpone the purchase until your comfort level increases in your ability to meet the expense and demand of the proposed new bill.

And, hey, if you had "zero" credit to begin with as was the presupposition of why you are reading this little manual, then you already know how to wait before buying an item. Waiting is a useful skill in this new credit score building game. Cultivate it until your resources tell you "Yes, now is the time to take advantage of this new opportunity."

STEP 7
TITHE TO SOMETHING
GIVE TO THE ORGANIZATION OR INDIVIDUAL OF YOUR CHOICE

What is tithing and how does it help me raise my credit score?

Without a dictionary definition, my idea of tithing is that one gives a certain portion of all he or she earns to a church religious group, charitable organization or a person that enriches his or her life in some meaningful way.

Generally, people tithe to a church or religious group. Still, you might ask: why would tithing be a step in a plan to raise a credit score or helping one to save thousands on future purchases?

I guess for me the deeper question when we talk about saving money boils down to a goal of having financial prosperity in your life and not just a better credit score.

Good to excellent credit scores are needed when you want to finance something at a low interest rate, but how sweet would it be to be in a position where you can pay cash for an expensive item and not even need to finance it.

Tithing, in my experience, is the very best way to raise your resources tenfold just by giving.

There may be arguments as to which type of giving brings the greatest return on investment, but there is little debate that one must give in order to receive.

Tithing to your church or religious organization is, in my opinion, the best way to give if you seek guaranteed returns, while tithing or giving to individuals or to those benevolent organizations that enrich your life in some way can be rewarding too.

Giving is important because it increases your feeling of well being by making you feel good. By giving, you are saying to the universe that you are already affluent and have so much that you can afford to give out to others.

For these reasons, I feel that tithing has to be a part of any financial plan aimed at providing you with financial prosperity, which--in the long run-- might really be what you are seeking, and not just a better credit score.

Step 7 -- Summary / To Do

Begin tithing on a regular basis to the group, person or organization of your choice.

Tithing is a component of all the great spiritual traditions and is linked inexplicably to the creation of wealth and abundance.

There is a method to tithing which when used can be measured as an immediate return on investment (ROI). And, while speaking in terms of an ROI as related to giving from the spirit may prove offensive to some, it has nonetheless been my experience that when you tithe with expectation of a return on your investment, your rewards are usually in line with your expectation.

To give, i.e. plant a seed, with no expectation of a return, i.e. for the seed to grow abundantly into a huge harvest, is not a logical thing to do.

All you need to do is give, expect and receive the harvest of your seed planting.

My best advice to you is not to analyze this ancient "seed/harvest" law if it is not something that you have tried in the past. Just start giving and begin experiencing the results for yourself.

STEP 8
TITHE TO YOURSELF

Reading the title of this step, you may have the same question: How does tithing to myself increase my ability to improve my credit score and save me thousands of dollars in my lifetime?

Once again, this step speaks to the underlying reason you might want to increase a credit score, and that reason is the same as in the previous step: mainly to become financially prosperous in life by going beyond just increasing numbers on a credit score page.

Let's face it: if you give yourself at least 10% of all you earn and put it in a monetary vehicle that adds to the principle, then that puts you in a better position financially.

It also subconsciously helps you to believe that you are worthy enough to have money to your name or in your name.

Though people may tithe to a religious organization without thinking about what comes back to them in the way of additional help and resources, very seldom does one put away 10% in a personal vault with his or her name on it without thinking about it. And I've concluded that it is the thinking about it, about the money, that you have as opposed to the money that you don't have that has the most beneficial effect on you.

From personal experience, I can say that once I started saving money for myself, it seems everything just got easier.

I set it up so that the money comes out of my paycheck automatically and every now and then--like every payday--I check the balance to see how much my little pot of gold has grown. Though I know that money is not equitable with my true self worth, nonetheless, I also know the world thinks otherwise. And so on a subconscious level, it helps me feel more worthy.

It is not a feeling one can describe but one that you must experience for yourself.

So, on your journey to having more, keeping more and saving more, tithing to yourself can be the missing link that makes it all worthwhile.

I now have a little money in a vault that has my name on it. This is money that grows and gets larger every month. I now feel more secure about weathering any storms that might cross my horizon. I can also use these self-tithing funds to fund some of my other dreams …dreams like owning a home in my retirement years or vacationing on different beaches throughout the world.

The sky becomes the limit when you learn and love to pay yourself at least as much as you love to give to others and pay your creditors.

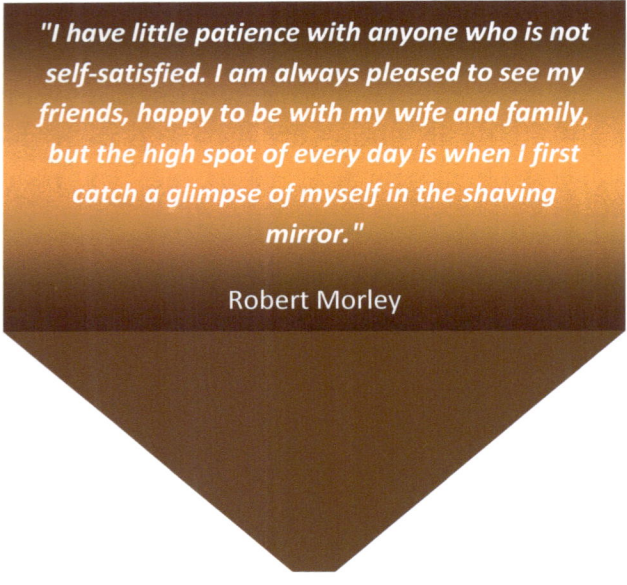

"I have little patience with anyone who is not self-satisfied. I am always pleased to see my friends, happy to be with my wife and family, but the high spot of every day is when I first catch a glimpse of myself in the shaving mirror."

Robert Morley

Step 8 -- Summary / To Do

Put Aside a Percentage of All You Earn in an Account Called "Me" to Increase Your Worthiness and Self Esteem

I have to admit that I am guilty of knowing but not using this "pay yourself first" principle for the almost two thirds of my life, but that is no reason not to put it into practice for the next 33 years of my life.

There's a book called *The Automatic Millionaire* by David Bach that I usually give to all the high school and college graduates in my family. In essence, the book shows the new graduate how to become a millionaire without much effort by using the law of compound interest over the course of the next 30 years of their life. Save just a little now and be a millionaire by the time you retire.

It is a noble goal and one that is achievable to anyone with time, discipline and the ability to put aside just a little money every paycheck.

This step, like the last one, has a try it for yourself label on it because the feelings it evokes cannot be described and the money you can acquire can only be experienced individually.

Take the plunge. Start your individual savings plan with your name on it today.

STEP 9
CREATE SOME RESIDUAL INCOME

Can you say "Residual income?"

The previous two chapters spoke more to achieving overall financial success, more so than just saving thousands that can come from raising your credit score.

Still, this is a guide for increasing what you get to keep as you live a life of giving and expecting a return on the seeds you scatter.

Of all the things I have learned regarding creating financial abundance, there is one thing that stands out in my belief system.

And that is if you trade time for money, there will one day come a time when you will either get tired of doing what you are doing or some other circumstance will cause you not to be able to do it any longer, be it old age or sickness or disability.

So, to assure your financial prosperity lasts beyond your working years, you will need to find some way to receive funds from investments, i.e. your money continuing to work for you long after you have stopped working or otherwise actively engaged in any income producing strategy.

There is a young man who is the son of a "Prepaid Legal" millionaire who published a little CD some years ago entitled "*17 Ways to Get Rich at Any Age Any Background.*" His name is Bryant Aucoin. In it, he talks about the difference between assets and liabilities in much the same way that Robert Kiyosaki talks about them in the book *Rich Dad Poor Dad.*

But the primary thing the CD does is discusses some 17 businesses that can throw off residual income to you and your estate when pursued in the right way. I encourage you to find the CD if you can.

Residual income is income that continues to put money in your pocket long after you have done the initial work or made the initial investment.

For example, I've written over 30 books in various niche markets. They are each one of them a way to put money in my pocket long after the writing is done.

As a more complete example, lets' say it takes me 10 hours to write this short book on how to increase your credit score based on my own experience with the process. If I sell 20 copies at $10 each, that's $200 dollars. And in this hypothetical example, let's say it was an eBook and there were no printing cost incurred by me as the writer.

In that example, I would have made $20 per hour in the writing of the book, selling just 20 copies. But what if I sell 20 copies each month for the next 10 months. I would then be up to 200 copies at $10 each, or $2000 for the writing of this small guide. That would put me up to $200 per hour in the writing of this manuscript, as measured by the traditional method of trading time for money. You would have to agree that this would not be a bad return for the initial time investment.

Such is the power of letting assets (i.e. the book) work for you, instead of you trading time for money.

Once I learned that I could never get rich trading time for money, I begun seeking ways to create and have assets working for me.

The practice has allowed me to survive and always be semi-retired, a luxury all people who desire it should enjoy.

So, the final piece of advice in your 9 Step Plan to saving more money and becoming financially independent is to do a little research and find a way to create some residual income for yourself.

By the way, once you get your own credit score in order and have all the credit your need, new ways to make money will begin to surface.

As a final example, I have to tell you that once I went in to sign the papers on my new used auto loan, the Credit Union representative said I can get your interest rate down from 2.44% to 2.24% if you bundle your loan with our Platinum credit card offer. I said "YES. Let's Do it!"

The credit card rate was 8.9% and came with perks of its own. Rewards like six months interest-free and even a transfer clause to allow transferring balances from higher interest rate cards.

Then one month later--while finishing up this little guide--I get an email telling me that the Credit Union really likes me and that they were lowering my credit card interest rate to 8.65%. It just keeps getting better and better with the Credit Union. None of my other banks has ever done that. Credit Unions rock.

It was only later that I came up with the idea of using this new line of credit to create more wealth assets for myself.

Maybe I'll buy another used car, let my mechanic friend fix it up and then flip it to make a profit.

Or, maybe I can use the funds to join an MLM (multi-level marketing company) I had been thinking about but did not previously have the funds to pursue. Maybe I'll sell the wares at the flea market or let someone else sell for me and split the profits.

Or, now that I know how to get my own credit in order, I'll help others do the same. Not everyone will want to repair his or her credit on his or her own. Maybe they will need help. Maybe I know a reputable company they can use .

Or, maybe… as you can see, the possibilities are endless. Having credit can change your financial future in a multitude of ways, including placing income producing, asset generating opportunities within reach.

You just need to act.

Either do it yourself or get the help you need from a reputable credit repair service.

Hopefully, these nine steps have given you the inspiration to get started on your journey to not only saving more money by having a higher credit score, but has also raised your awareness on how to become even more financially successful using any new credit at your disposal.

In the final (optional) chapter, I summarize all the details of my own "From Zero to 778 Credit Score in 15 months," story. It may not be your journey, but you might gain some insights on the pitfalls to avoid while journeying to the top of the credit score ladder.

Good luck to you as you reach your goal as easily and as quickly as possible while pedaling downstream.

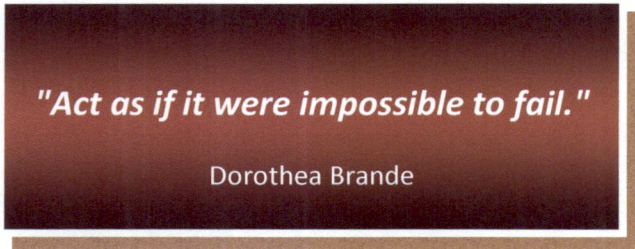

MY PERSONAL JOURNEY "FROM ZERO TO 778 IN 15 MONTHS" STORY

I am an "older" bird, so I will not take you all the way back to the beginning. That would take too long, so I will start 22 years ago in 1995 when I left the country to serve as a volunteer for a religious organization in Haifa Israel.

When I left the country that year, my credit score was not that great. I remember only having a little bit of funds left on a credit card as small emergency provision for my overseas journey.

Being away for over five years actually helped my credit. I suppose because I was not adding fuel to the fire with any new delinquent accounts, so it was all good.

When I returned in late 2000, my credit score had probably improved. I did not know how much until I went to buy a new car in 2002. I got the car with zero money down, coming off an upside down car loan on a vehicle that had just had a transmission overhaul.

I was working full time, earning less than $40,000 a year, but found that I could qualify for a new home if I had $500 to $1000 on hand. Therefore, I did what any self-respecting woman would do: I asked my brothers to chip in, and one of my good friends offered help as well.

So in the space of a year, I had a new car to drive and a new condominium to live in.

I remember thinking I needed to buy a home so that I could settle down. Until that point, I had been wandering not only all over the country, but had lived on three different continents to boot.

But, staying in the Atlanta area was not to be. When my supervisor retired at the state agency I was working at, she was replaced by someone who I considered to be a bigot and a racist.

So I left my condominium, moved to Raleigh, NC

and worked that same job there for another year. In the meantime, I was trying to keep up payments on the condominium, support expenses in a new apartment and the expenses of both eventually became over-whelming.

I eventually sold the condominium in a "short sell" thinking that would have less impact on my credit worthiness. I remember how painful it was throughout the process of not being able to meet my expenses.

Did I say yet that I was in mid-life crises as well and would no longer tolerate injustice in my immediate work environment? At the time, I was working my 8 to 5 state job as a disability examiner and the organization was not as well managed as it could have been. Certainly not as well managed as the agency I had left. When I complained to the Director that something needed to be changed so examiners would have the support and tools they needed to do their job and not be overwhelmed with stacks and stacks of cases on their desks, it was met with some degree of compassion, but the change was slow to come and by then I had had enough.

So I left that job -- and though my co-workers who were just as overwhelmed said I would never qualify for unemployment if I left -- I, nonetheless, got unemployment benefits, primarily because my UE caseworker had read the story in the paper years before and seen how the examiners' desks were stacked with multitudes of cases with no end in sight.

What does all that have to do with Credit Scores? Well, when I became unemployed, not only did my salary decrease, but my ability to pay my bills decreased too.

By 2007, I was back at home, living with my mother and other folks, and threatening to write a social security disability book so that not all that disability examiner training would be wasted.

In the meantime, I lived in a "cash only" economy from 2007 to 2017 because I knew or suspected no one would give me credit for anything.

In those 10 years, I worked a full time job for almost a year, then worked the Census Bureau in 2010 for a few months full time, but other than that, I was never employed full time. With me being in my 50s, I was unwilling to keep sending out resume after resume online with no responses, so I gave all that madness up. If someone said there is not age discrimination in the job market, I am afraid I would have to disagree.

Luckily, in 2008 or 2009, my sister had an extra car that she was not using and gave it to me to look for work and get around. I did look for part time work and begun writing books to create some residual income.

And yes, I was living on less than $5000 a year but I did not let that stop me from traveling to Israel in 2001 for a special event, or from going back on a nine-day Pilgrimage in 2011. Life continued uninterrupted in a "cash" economy with me relying more and more on the "law of attraction" and tithing as a means of meeting my expenses (but that is another book entirely).

Then, after eight years, in 2016 when my 1997 Toyota was approaching 300,000 miles, I realized I needed to begin thinking about how I would replace it when the time came.

So I did what you might do: I went to a car dealership to see what, if anything they could do for me. That was in April 2016. It was then that I learned that I had a "zero" credit score. There was absolutely nothing on my credit report. And, as they say, sometimes having a zero score is worst then having a bad score. There was no history of anything on that report.

The man at the local Nissan dealership was kind and politely told me that my best course of action was to join a credit union so I could start to rebuild my credit. It was good advice and only after the application for the loan did I start to receive the seven or eight rejection notices in the mail weeks afterwards.

At that point, I knew I needed to try to find at least a part time job. I had some residual monthly income from the books I had written, and by February 2017, I had gotten a part time job working 12-14 hours a week.

When I finally got the internal nudge that it was time to look for a car after a $200 bill that came from getting my vehicle to pass inspection in April, I was keeping an eye on my credit score at Credit Karma.

When my score went over 650, I decided it was time to apply for that car. So I did. Told the credit union what I wanted to pay for a used car and asked them to give me a $10,000 loan. Though my net yearly income was still under $10K a year, I knew that I needed a car, and that if I did not ask, I could not receive.

The credit union took a long time to respond. Maybe

because it was summer and people were taking vacations, I am not sure of the cause. When I finally heard from them, they told me they would give me the money, had been working on a way to get me the funds on the monthly payment terms that I wanted, and that I had one week to find a car using the credit score that they had approved the loan under. I later learned that score was 703.

My intuition told me I had to find my $10K car inside the week or there may be problems. I did not question this internal feeling, but instead went to find my car.

I test drove and fell in love with a 2012 Nissan Murano, but it was outside my budget. Keep in mind that I was now buying a car that I really had no budget for. The car was coming two months before I had set up my new membership site that I had been trying to work on. This site was being built to bring in the additional $200 per month needed for my new used car. So, at that time, there was no budget for this car no matter at what interest rate I obtained.

The Credit Union had approved my loan with a 2.44% interest rate and I thought that was outstanding. On the day that I went to sign the papers, they told me they could lower that to 2.24%, if I would package it with a new credit card. I agreed.

In the end, my payment ended up being $16 per month over my non-existent budget amount because I elected to get a four-year power train warranty on my new used Lincoln MKX. I suspected I would not have the funds to fix this 10-year-old car if something major went wrong, and the warranty helped to set my mind at ease.

As to my intuition to find the car in the seven days, I had been right about that too. Turns out, the same weekend I acquired the car, an old unpaid medical bill showed up on my credit report and affected my credit score negatively.

So, being proactive, I later contacted the debt collector to see if they would remove the statement from my credit report if I paid the bill, to which they replied that it would not be up to them but the original debtor. Hey, I tried to give them the money, but without the guarantee of removal from my credit report, I had no incentive to pay them off early, which I could have done easily with my BRAND NEW CREDIT CARD!

Hey, I know you may be working with more money than I was working with as I attempted to improve my credit. Having insufficient income was a major obstacle with all the other creditors who might have supplied my loan. However, by being a member of a credit union--which was not even in my county-- this was my ace in the hole. I had been honest with them from day one when I opened the account. I had told them I wished to reestablish my credit and had asked them to help by loaning me $500 as a personal secured loan. They kept their part of the deal by loaning me the money, and I kept mine by paying them back in six months at an interest rate that was so low, it boggles the mind as to how they could do it. I think I paid something like $3 or $6 in interest over the course of the six-months, $500 loan.

Now, with the car out of the way, my next goal is to continue to maintain and improve my credit score, to somehow increase my income, and to purchase a nice little home for me to retire in by the beach somewhere.

Because of my low-income status--which could and should improve--I must buy a home rather than live in an apartment because frankly it will be cheaper than apartment living once it has all been said and done.

Here is the final piece to my story. After I bought the car, I applied to change my cell phone company. They sent me a credit report notice saying I would require a deposit. The credit score they had listed on the notice was ... wait ... wait ... wait on it ...wait...**778**! Dang. Seems like no deposit would be required with that nice score, but oh well. Maybe I would have gotten a pardon if they had only known just how far I had come.

So from applying for a car in April 2016 to actually purchasing a car in July 2017, I went from a credit score of virtually ZERO to 778.

The content of this little book tells you how I did it, and how you can do it too by following the suggestions in the summaries following each chapter.

This book does not discuss how one with bad credit can improve your score. For that, I would follow the recommendations inside CreditKarma.com or use a reputable credit repair service. And yes, I do have one in mind I can refer you to.

Questions still about how to go from Zero to 778 in 15 months? Hit me up and I will answer, but it may be easier just to open a CreditKarma.com account and follow its suggestions and advice on how to best improve your score with simple actions that are designed to improve your credit worthiness.

All the best to you in your journey to save thousands

In interest rate charges on your next major purchase, whether it is a new car, your starter home or your dream home.

ABOUT THE AUTHOR

Loretta Crosby has written and published more than 30 titles in various niches. Titles under her name include *Getting Social Security Disability: Your 9 Step Individual Action Plan* and a book of poetry entitled *Talking Walls and Spirit Calls*. She resides in North Carolina and plans to retire on an east coast beach in order to devote more time to writing, living and serving.

Catch her online at facebook.com/onepupil9 and twitter.com/onepupil9

SERVE...BLESS...INSPIRE...PURPOSE!

"Success is not the result of spontaneous combustion. You must set yourself on fire."

Reggie Leach

www.ingramcontent.com/pod-product-compliance
Lightning Source LLC
Chambersburg PA
CBHW040241220526
45473CB00001B/328